Falling Into Love:
Reflections Along the Path

Falling Into Love

Reflections Along The Path

Margaret Rosche

Hughes Henshaw Publications   2005

Copyright © 2005 Margaret Rosche

All rights reserved, including the right to reproduce this book or portions thereof in any form whatsoever. For information:

Hughes Henshaw Publications
424 Hurst Road NE
Palm Bay, FL 32907

Library of Congress Cataloging-in-Publication Data

Rosche, Margaret
    Falling Into Love: Reflections Along the Path

1. Poems, 2. Spiritual life — Miscellanea, 3. God — Miscellanea 4. Relationships — Miscellanea I. Title

ISBN 1-892698-12-7

Cover image by Karen E. Wood

Cover design by Christina

Manufactured in the United States of America

For information regarding special discounts for bulk purchases, please contact Hughes Henshaw Publications Special Sales at: 1-321-956-8885 and hugheshenshaw@aol.com

CONTENTS

DEDICATION　vii

THANKSGIVING　viii

INTRODUCTION　xvii

PART ONE: REDEMPTION　1

GOODBYE AT THE THIRD GREEN　5
HELP YOURSELF　6
RESURRECTION　8
RIVER WASH　10
STILL IN US　12
THE HOME IN MY HEART　13
THERE YOU ARE　14

PART TWO: THE YEAR I GAVE UP MEN　17

LOVING　21
RETURN TO MACHU PICHU　22
THE GIFT　23
THE MAN IN MY HEAD　24
THE YEAR I GAVE UP MEN　27
THELMA'S SONG　31
WHO WILL LOVE ME NOW?　32

PART THREE: WALKING TO JERUSALEM 35

A DARK AND STORMY NIGHT 39
ANNUNCIATION 40
APPOINTMENT AT MACHU PICCHU 42
AWAKENING 44
BECOMING ORCHESTRAL 47
BIGGER 50
DO IT ANYWAY 51
CALLING IN 52
COME AWAY 54
FALLEN ANGEL 56
GOD IN MY GLASS 58
HAPPY NOW 60
RIDING THE GREAT WHITE 63
IN RELUCTANT PRAISE OF BIBLE STUDY 64
PIECES OF YOU 66
QUEEN OF HEARTS 68
SATIS 70
THE QUESTION 72
WANTING LESS 74
WASHING DAD 76
WHAT TO DO? 78

PART FOUR: I AM THE ONE 81

PAINTING PEACE 85
I AM, AREN'T I? 86
YOU ARE: I AM 88
NOW WHEN 90
STORM SONG 91
JUST FOR ME 92
SACRED ME 94
EXCLAIM! 95
THERE AND BACK 96
VASE 97

PART FIVE:
PRAYERS, SONGS AND BLESSINGS   99

ALWAYS AFFIRMATIONS   103
ANGEL LOVE: MICHAEL'S SONG   104
BLESS THIS HOUSE   105
CHANT   106
AFFIRMATIONS FOR A CHURCH   108
GODDESS BIRTHDAY BLESSING   110
HAIL WOMAN   111
I DO   112
LITANY I: MOTHER GOD   114
LITANY II: ONE WOMAN   116
LABYRINTH PRAYER   117
OUR SOURCE I   118
OUR SOURCE II   120
OFFERING   121
PRAYER FOR LIVING   122
RELATIONSHIP INVOCATION.   124
SEAMLESS: TOM'S SONG   125
SINGING YOU HOME: A CELEBRATION   126
THE OVERFLOWING CUP   128
WEDDING SONG   129
LITANY III: WOMAN PRAYER   130

EPILOGUE: MEMORIAL FOR THE AUTHOR   **132**

BENEDICTION   **135**

SOURCES AND INSPIRATION   **136**

ABOUT THE AUTHOR   **139**

The
Real love
I always keep a secret.

All my words
Are sung outside his window,
For when he lets me in
I take a thousand oaths of silence.

But then he says,

O, then God says,

"What the hell, Maggie,
Why not give the whole world
My address."

Hafiz
What The Hell
(adapted)
from
*The Gift: Poems By Hafiz
The Great Sufi Master*

Guy C. Simpson
September 28, 1938 – February 12, 2000

Then through my hell of helplessness,
I felt an unseen presence press,
And when I rose it lingered on,
And still the glory is not gone.

James Dillet Freeman
Still The Glory Is Not Gone
(excerpt)
from
Love Is Strong as Death

DEDICATION

This book is dedicated to Guy C. Simpson, my husband and friend, who made his transition in February of 2000.

I always remember him as the personification of roguish good humor, eyes sparkling with devilish charm. But he was also gentle, funny, caring, thoughtful, and sensitive, the darling of women, children, cats, and dogs wherever he went. They *knew*.

He was the best of men, my beloved, a Canadian citizen, and salt of the earth of our two countries. He was lover, companion, teacher, catalyst, inspiration, and burr under my saddle. He nurtured my growth even in death as grief became fertile ground for the working of Spirit. I have no doubt our great adventure together was lovingly planned by mutual consent long ago at some celestial conference table.

I am grateful for our eighteen years of abundant life together, and for the *me* that evolved from our experience as partners. I met him when I was sorely in need of redemption. Challenged by a failed first marriage and years of exploratory single-hood, I had all but given up on the possibility of sustainable intimacy with the opposite sex.

Back then, the consolations of conscious spiritual seeking were far in the future. Organized religion seemed to me an exploitative mix of adulterated history, blatant opportunism, and shiny new-age fantasy. Guy's simple, honest love stopped me in my type-A tracks, slowed the pace of an over-thought life, and created the safe space I needed to pay attention to both myself and Spirit. Together we were able to explore emotional intimacy and the unexpected possibility of *happily ever after*.

Perhaps my relationship with Guy is best summed up by a Valentine letter I wrote to his daughter's preteen children in February of 2001, the first anniversary of his death.

Dear Courtney and Ryan:

I am still very sad, but I thought I might use the occasion of Valentine's Day to share with you why I loved your Grampa, the way he made me feel, and why I miss him so much.

Ryan, he was a strong and sensitive man who laughed and cried, who both sheltered me and let me be my own person. You could do worse than to model yourself after him. I sense that you have inherited some of his sensitivity and tenderness, and that is a very good thing.

Courtney, he was a companion and a friend as well as a husband. We laughed a lot, which is so important. He cared for me when I was sick, upset, or "bitchy," as well as during the fun times. I hope you will find a life companion you enjoy "just being with" as much as I enjoyed being with Grampa Guy.

I hope this helps you see what a wonderful person he was...as a man, friend, husband, and role model for both of you. I hope you can also feel, even a little, what a good thing it is to find someone who loves you back in this special way.

After only ten years together, simultaneous life-threatening illnesses challenged both our lives and our marriage. My own near-death and his eight year struggle with heart failure and stroke introduced me to the most transformative roles of my life. It also handily set the stage for my continued awakening from a long, self-absorbed dream to a new understanding of life, death and purpose.

To this day I am convinced we have loved, played, and parted before, and will probably act out our healing drama again. I feel we came together this time so that he might unceremoniously nudge me further along my path. In retrospect, I know the heart of the matter was that our loving allowed me the freedom and security to expand inward, continue remembering who I am, and open to my Higher Self. In fact, I often wonder if this was not, for me, the primary reason for our relationship.

So, thank you, honey. I often think of what you said just two days before you left, relaxed in the hot tub, sipping our favorite wine. Your words became a parting gift for me to treasure:
> *"It doesn't get any better than this."*

Where does the real poetry
Come from?

From the amorous sighs
In the moist dark when making love
With form or
Spirit.

Where does poetry live?

In the eye that says, "Wow wee."
In the overpowering felt splendor
Every sane mind knows
When it realizes – our life dance
Is only for a few magic
Seconds.

From the heart saying,
Shouting,

"I am so damn
Alive."

Wow
from
*The Gift: Poems By Hafiz
The Great Sufi Master*

Ryan, Guy, and Courtney: magic moment.

We cannot have a spiritual life
that is completely separate
from our corporeal selves.
We need to see one another,
to touch and be touched,
to exchange some gift, some energy,
some knowing that can only be
transmitted in the physical body,
from one to another.
It is tangible, yet mystical;
physical, yet immeasurable, invisible.

Wayne Muller
How Then Shall We Live

THANKSGIVING

My gratitude goes, first, to Spirit for the blessings and creativity which continue to flow through me in extraordinary ways.

And now is the appropriate time to thank those people who have enjoyed my work over the years and expressed variations on this theme to me: *"You know, you should really think of publishing this."*

Of course, huge thanks go to publisher Daphna Moore for being there when I was finally ready to roll, to poetry editor Beverly Sweet for sharpening my instrument, and to graphic artist Karen Wood for her evocative depiction of the Daytona Beach moon that rose "just for me."

Thank you to my mother, who taught me to love early in my life; to my father, who taught me to love late in his; to my sister, Louise, who is my heart; and to my brother-in-law, Santos, for being such a whole man. My nurturing family of origin anchors, and sustains the personal me with their *every-day-is-Christmas* kind of love.

Heartfelt thanks also to Judith, Kay, Lori, Therese, Sonja, Jenny, and to all my precious friends, prayer partners, and extended family; for nurturing, stimulating, inspiring and re-creating me in countless ways. You are the filet mingnon, mashed potatoes, and crème brulee of my creative process.

Thank you, of course, to Unity Church, its founders, ministers, teachers, poets, and seekers, for being the particular voice of Spirit which spoke my language and pointed the way home. With special thanks to John Anderson, Robert Brumet, Darlene Capinah, Pam Fenn, James Dillet Freeman, Paul Hasselbeck, Beth Head, James Rosemergy, Sky St. John, Charles Turner, and Rose Whitham. You ground my dance.

Many thanks also to Abraham, Ellen Bass, Joseph Benner, Deepak Chopra, Wayne Dyer, Hafiz, Meister Eckhart, Kryon, Wayne Muller, Penney Peirce, Gary Renard, ,Rumi, Seth, Mattie Stepanek, Francis of Assisi, Neal Donald Walsh, A Course in Miracles, and the myriad other inspired writers, poets, rebels, angels, and mystics, embodied or otherwise, who have lifted and booted me along my path.

In poems, joy and sorrow are mates.
They lie down together,
their hands all over each other...
...their sexes fitting seamlessly as day and night.
They arch over us,
glistening and bucking,
the portals through which we enter our lives.

Everything On The Menu
(excerpt)
from
Mules For Love: Poems By Ellen Bass

INTRODUCTION

The poems in this book are snapshots of my journey. They are slices of experience; beginnings, endings, blessings, challenges, confusions, revelations, deaths, rebirths; each a part of my evolving relationship with Higher Self. You may call this process by whatever name resonates with your own journey toward meaning. For me it is the excavation of God-in-me from under layers of ego disguises, personae, roles, and paradigms, assiduously collected during 59 years of uproarious life in my body.

The subject is, I suppose, love. At depth, it is about impersonal primal Love, the substance of who we are, the stuff scientists call the essence of our physical universe. Other names for it are God, Principle, Pure Being, the Tao, the Universe, Higher Self, All-That-Is, the One, I AM, or the Un-nameable. I've even heard it called "George". It doesn't really matter what we call it: What I know, intuitively and increasingly now, scientifically, is that **It is**….and, therefore, so am I, and you, and everything else in our inner and outer space.

In this visible world, falling is one of the human infant's primal fears. By adulthood, falling became a fact of life for me. I tripped over my own feet, stumbled into trouble, and slipped on banana peels left on the path by life. I was pushed over the edge, thrown out of windows, bungee jumped for the thrill of it, and parachuted to save my life. In fact, I found myself taking any number of physical, emotional and psychological falls (Does *falling in love* sound familiar?). All involved elements of fear, risk, loss of control, and surrender, willing or unwilling, to the unknown.

Once I found that human love and love objects are fallible and transitory at best, my falls took on a deeper significance. They were the means to open me to primal Love instead of fear; to what life is all about...what I am all about. Surrender became trust, an opportunity to engage Higher Self, connect with Love as essence, and meet my infallible, eternal Spirit. The path may not be easy, but it is, ultimately, the road back to Love, and the only way to go to healing and wholeness, to *heaven*. *Falling Into Love* describes the process of waking up to my individual life as an expression of transcendent LIFE, and of me allowing Love to pour Itself out into the world, both through me and as me.

God-lets of being, mortal cups overflowing with unique expressions of the One perfect Love...that's what I *feel* we are. The ultimate relationship has become, for me, that of myself with the One, with pure Love, pure Being. This reciprocal partnership seduces me into exploration, for therein lies the answer to all questions, the end point of all quests. The more I search, the more I realize my identity in Spirit, *as* Spirit, and the more I find references, allusions to, and illustrations of that truth in the most unlikely places; ancient, modern, sacred, profane, hidden, and in-my-face. I was recently astonished that a dusty saint of my conservative Catholic childhood, medieval mystic, Francis of Assisi, neatly summed it up for me with these words:

"What we are looking for is what is looking."

Exactly. We are pieces of God searching for It-self, for wholeness, for the One from which we emanate, exploring, expanding, and growing into our *God-ness* as we progress.

For me, progress has meant the challenge of evolution, a progression of daily, sometimes moment-to-moment journeys toward self *re*-definition. I am learning to define myself in relation to Spirit, to real Love first instead of in reference to someone or some thing outside of me, starting over each time I forget. Today I focus on maintaining a functional primary relationship with Spirit. Preserving this essential union has become a lifetime commitment.

Lest you think that my initial *a-ha*, had anything to do with planning or volition, think again. I was dragged, kicking and screaming into awareness! My ego's defenses needed to be breached by a rather large set of cosmic two-by-fours. Actually, it was more like demolition of the fort than a breach in my defenses.. I almost lost everything that mattered to me, including my own life, before I slowed down enough to see what really mattered, to *see* things differently. It changed my life.

Here are some of my thoughts, feelings, and insights along the path I am dancing toward enlightenment. My inspiration comes from night and day-dreams, meditation, communing with nature, prayer, and other forms of Light shot into the busy consortium of my waking consciousness. Whole poems or seed fragments have dropped into my head like apples from a tree. When that happens, I write. Some of the offerings are solemn, some mystical, some celebratory, others whimsical. It is my sincere wish that you enjoy them and, perhaps, be heartened, awakened, inspired, and amused.

In any event, it has been my pleasure.

Part One

Redemption

All your images of winter
I see against your sky.

I understand the wounds
That have not healed in you.

They exist
Because God and love
Have not yet become real enough

To allow you to forgive
The dream.

Forgive The Dream
(excerpt)
from
*The Gift: Poems by Hafiz
The Great Sufi Master*

As you regain the peace of God
it will eventually result in the ability
to reclaim your natural state of joy
regardless of what appears
to be happening in the world.

Gary R. Renard
The Disappearance of the Universe

Swear not to die, you holy sons of God!

A Course In Miracles

GOODBYE AT THE THIRD GREEN

Tonight your kin
return you to the elements;
native soil,
lush rain-soaked green,
murmuring brook,
sun setting low
over misty mounds.

Eight perfect roses bob downstream.
Your children and their children,
two fathers and your wife,
lay you gently
where you loved to be.

Your daughter wades in,
bending to release you to the stream;
last request finally honored,
final farewells lovingly spoken,
soft prayers in the twilight hush.

And tomorrow and tomorrow
old friends and new
will roll over Number Three,
silently saluting you
with their love of the game.

HELP YOURSELF

Family, friends:
serve platters of Love
with all the trimmings,
this holiday,
baskets of gratitude heaped high
with the plain and simple joy
of feasting on life with each other.

I was hungry all my life
for love seasoned with friendship,
sweetened with peace and purpose.

Young love teased
with tastes,
youthful passion
with the aroma,
of banquets to come
with him.

Memories of love
nourish, sustain me.
My cup ran over so often
with this good man,
I have good to spare,
plenty to share.
Our feast of love feeds me still,
and I am grateful.

So please,
help yourself.

RESURRECTION

Fantastic fortune:
despair foretells rebounding joy,
hopeless wound bleeds hopeful peace.

Unlatched by grief,
the jewel box of my life opens,
well of native elegance,
wide and deep,
richly carved with stories
and this latest raw, weeping drama.

Inside;
light-born treasure,
immortal magic,
gems streaming glory
into my darkest day.

Grief-bloated events press close around,
but cannot mask what lives inside.
This turn of the wheel grinds me fine,
fills my emptiness.
New loaves grow me,
move me on.

Dry daily bread transforms to feast,
sorrow to rarest gold,
impotent anger to silver surrender.
My plate is full.

I plumb Source,
plunging deep the hands of my heart
in purest play,
claiming coal squeezed to diamond,
the hard-won,
precious stones of experience.

Nurtured awake,
freed from grief by joy,
from death by abundant Life,
I dress for dinner.

Clothed in peace,
I put on love,
and
suitably attired,
live forever.

RIVER WASH

"Take me to the river...wash me in the water...."
**He would have loved that silly, singing fish
and laughed.**

A year has passed without his laughter.
I have lived on sorrow's shore,
washed up by loneliness
beached by loss.

In the beginning, grief was swollen, flood-stage.
It covered our two countries, another ocean.
Bottomless, it seemed.
I drowned in memory.

Later, grief merely raged, defined me:
washed, tumbled, tossed,
heart and soul-sick,
one-half of nothing.

Flung ashore in a new place,
I found a different me,
stranger to myself,
remade by love and loss.

At times, I sailed again into the waning storm,
let lightning strike, to die again with him,
waded shallows of sadness,
aching to remember.

I learned to
bathe myself more gently in tear-laced water,
float a new boat,
trail touch-hungry fingers in healing love.

The world drew me back,
lifesaving connection,
redeeming, healing.
The river narrowed, ebbed to cherished memory.

But I have saved a bit of that pure water,
to taste the truth of life with him,
splash drops of "us"
on dusty single-hood.

I am more whole for his gift of self.
And surely we have loved and parted times before,
will love again,
love even now.

"I've been to the river... washed me in the water...."
My honey loves that silly, singing fish
and he laughs!

STILL IN US:
FOR HIS CHILDREN

He is gone,
his smile, his arms,
reduced to ash and bone.
Love and kisses, joys and pains,
are memories we own.

He is in you,
flesh and blood,
youth and hope fulfilled.
In your children you can see his
essence playing still.

He is in me,
our dream complete,
though now we are apart.
Our time of soulful loving lives
forever in my heart.

We are one,
a family
of more than flesh and bone.
He did not die, he lives in us,
and only left for home.

THE HOME IN MY HEART

My dear, I sold the house today,
not just this one, but two;
the house up north, our home right here.
Goodbye once more to you.

The places where we lived and loved,
made marriage and a life,
shared blessings, love and laughter,
challenges, and strife.

O Canada, beloved home,
fireflies along the path.
Children play forever young,
remembering grampa's laugh.

America, the beautiful,
was proud to welcome you:
husband, second father's son,
friend, brother, uncle. True.

My dear, I sold the house today.
It's time to let that lie.
Your home is now inside my heart
where there is no goodbye.

THERE YOU ARE

I reach out: you're not here.
Wracked with grief,
life is stark.

I curse death, life and God.
Who will hold me
in the dark?

I disconnect,
close around empty arms,
shut down tight,

I stop here:
empty… silent…
healing in my soul's dark night.

And I hear silence shouting:
daughter, close your eyes
and see!

Now I feel…throb of essence…
one vibration.
Death melts into All-ness…free.

Clothed in Presence,
I let go to holy Oneness,
open up the sacred me.

There you are! my beloved.
All beloveds joined forever.
It is so….the sacred we.

Part Two

The Year I Gave Up Men

if you accept that the relationship
is here to make you conscious
instead of happy,
…the relationship will offer you salvation,
and you will be aligning yourself with
the higher consciousness
that wants to be born into this world.

Eckhart Tolle
Practicing the Power of Now

The purpose of a relationship
is to decide what part of yourself
you'd like to see "show up,"
not what part of another you can
capture and hold.

Neal Donald Walsh
Meditations From Conversations With God: Book 1

As you learn to see the fullness of
God's life and love and substance in others,
you will know that you need not
pour out your own for them.
You will have the knowledge and the Light
to call their attention to what they have
and prompt them to use it.

Myrtle Fillmore
Healing Letters

LOVING

I
am
grateful,
full of praise,
for human love.
C a r n a l wonder:
p a s s I o n a t e bodies
press toward the I n f I n I t e,
sacred-human vessels of love,
heat-seeking missiles of d e l i g h t.

Together we launch heaven or hell,
sweet salvation or conflagration.

We dance our dance of me,
and you, and us,
always coming
a r o u n d
again
to

Love.

RETURN TO MACHU PICCHU

**In loving memory of Margaret Canova
who scaled the sacred mountain
the year before her death at age 90**

Welcome home, venerable woman,
good news bearer, pillar of the church,
dispenser of coffee with caring and cream,
you sweetened our lives with Spirit and wit
as we drank your cup of joy.

Welcome back, Pachamama.
Then and now, you sit, serene,
the magic city at your feet.
Gods and children fill your lap
with reverent gifts
as you drink the sweet tea of eternal life.

Welcome Home, sister-friend, truth-keeper:
now you top the height of your dreams.
Outrageously pert,
you wave us upward to our refreshment,
while you sit, smoking, with your God.

THE GIFT

Love circles around to bless us all
in elegant, divine accord;
mothers, brothers, sisters, dads
partners, friends, and me, oh Lord.

We share tears, laughter, love,
the "comfort food" that loving brings.
Our circle grows both deep and wide.
It soothes, it hugs, it heals, it sings.

It dances, jingles, beats a drum,
claps, leaps up to touch the light.
feels warm and fuzzy, safe and free,
tucked in, filled up, complete, held tight.

Love gathers us together when
raging storms howl at the door.
It holds a hand, it wipes a tear,
when not-enough is asked for more.

Now this gift returns to you,
the love we share, to you from me,
because you touch my heart and life,
because you are my family.

THE MAN IN MY HEAD

Though I have made some progress
in screening what I'm fed,
there's still a man who lives in dreams
deep inside my head.

I fear there is a part of me
who still believes he'll come
to bear me off on his white horse,
a man who is " the one."

He's rolled up in a Persian rug,
he hides in castle towers,
he swings from vines, slays dragons fierce,
writes poetry, brings flowers.

And isn't that a fully loaded
flatbed truck he tows,
complete with rose-filled garden
and white picket-fenced abode?

Just when I thought I'd rooted out
those "ever after " stories,
up jumps the devil in a tale
of rescued maiden glories.

Or when I'm sitting, still and calm,
focused on I-Am,
my small self screams,
Yeah, 'be here now?!' Get real and find a man!

I try to purify my thoughts
but find, against my will,
it is collective consciousness
I'm making love to still.

Old paradigms are slow to die,
and tough to shake, it's true.
"Get swept away" may still show up
on lists of things to do.

Only constant practice keeps
my ego disconnected.
I pray, I read, I meditate,
until real Love's perfected,

until I see that *I* am Love,
and need not look outside;
until I learn *I* make the Love
that opens my heart wide.

I affirm my own true Love
Is here and now in me,
in family, friends, and in the world
I make by how I *see*.

Today I celebrate the Love
I can't get from another,
and find that when I come from there,
I truly love my brother.

Next time I see him charging in
to save himself or me,
I'll kill Prince Charming on the road,
and set both of us free!

Instead, I see myself, not him,
astride a noble steed,
a queen upon my own high horse
with everything I need.

And if, perhaps, together
toward the sunset we may ride,
I know our happy ending is
the Love we claim inside.

THE YEAR I GAVE UP MEN

Extraordinary, incendiary,
world-on-fire event,
super-consciousness expanding:
the year I gave up men.

A different way to view them,
that was the trick, you see.
Buying all that I'd been taught
just had not worked for me.

A small girl walked in daddy's steps
and danced upon his shoes,
but when I tried to walk his walk
he said *That's not for you!*

Men will protect you, do not fret.
They'll care for you, my girl.
He smiled and hugged me as he said,
It's not a woman's world.

I watched men come and go,
and conquer everything in sight.
Father, heroes, school boys, cowboys,
proving might-makes right.

They took the world my father owned
and took me on the side.
Inside-out and upside-down:
I was not satisfied.

The ride was bumpy, wild and hard,
a ride that was to be
to where I did not want to go,
to someone just not me.

It was addiction, predilection,
a hurt I *had* to have,
with love a war I could not win,
and wounds I could not salve.

I wanted them, needed them,
chased them around the bend.
Without them I was never whole,
until I gave up men.

I gave them up as band-aids,
toys and handymen.
I let go all the memories
of bad times way-back-when.

I became compassionate,
opened up to see,
and as I watched them operate
I saw they were like me.

I gave respect, said *You're OK,*
and ceased to throw the book.
I saw we are the same inside,
took a kinder look.

I found that it is *me* that shapes
the way I look at *us.*
All contention disappears
when I control the fuss

I took a stand for what I need,
but did not fire a shot.
I found I must make peace with me:
I get just what I've got.

Yes, I mourned the way I was
like somebody was dying,
that old familiar tug of war,
the passion and the crying.

I'd moaned "why me?" I'd pined for love
I'd cursed men, God, and fate.
It took some time to change my mind
and finally get it straight.

I rooted out old dos and don'ts,
the fairy tales and hype.
I put aside what mama said,
re-thought my stereotypes.

I gave up what I thought I knew
about men, love, and me,
I understood I make the love
that sets both of us free.

Men can't complete or redeem me.
That's no way to live.
I must heal and save me first,
then love them and forgive.

When I live right here and now,
when I raise the bar,
there is no contest, right or wrong
I simply know…*We Are.*

Extraordinary, incendiary,
heart-on-fire event:
I stopped, I looked, I saw us One,
the year I gave up men.

THELMA'S SONG

Lush bed of talents,
fenced but uncontained;
taste of truth,
sense of Spirit,
rush of goddess energy.

Truth and beauty flow, unstoppable;
stir souls,
trouble waters,
hide blessings
in plain sight.

We eye cloistered blooms,
lay blossoms at
heart-felt boundaries;
in awe, in tribute,
in solidarity.

Communion of gardeners,
soulful landscapers,
play in the mud until fences dissolve
and we become
one
perfect rose.

WHO WILL LOVE ME NOW?

If there are no accidents,
what do we learn
when we meet?

Restless minds,
hungry hearts
empty arms,
cunning instruments
of delight.

Seek, find;
win, lose;
run away, and back.

Yearn,
churn inside-out.

Try, shy,
quest, test,
shame, blame,
dance around
the only burning question.

Who will love me
now?

What are we?
Lovers, friends?
Predators?

Do we wish to kill the beast
just yet?

Sacrifice one for the other?

Do you even think such thoughts
inside yourself?

Such different worlds,
our separate selves.
Conniving to touch,
choking on pain.

And always
the question burns.
Who will love me?
Now.

Part Three

Walking To Jerusalem

There are no reference points.
The life story that has apparently happened
is uniquely and exactly
appropriate for each awakening.
All is just as it should be right now....
simply because all...is divine expression.

Tony Parsons
in
365 Nirvana Here And Now

I may be small, you may be tall,
But inside we are the same
Length of strength.

Mattie J.T. Stepanek
Rolter's Wisdom
in
Hope Through Heartstrings

So what is your intention now?
Do you intend to prove your theory
that life seldom brings you what you choose?
Or do you intend to demonstrate
Who You Are and
Who I Am?

Neal Donald Walsh
Meditations From Conversations With God: Book 1

Only when we leave
the amusement park of our mind
can we enter reality.

Robert Rabbin
in
365 Nirvana Here And Now

A DARK AND STORMY NIGHT

It is a dark and stormy night.
I wrestle adders of addiction, torrents of want,
reel through rutted fields of ego,
twisted roots of relating,
steaming swamps of emotion.

Spent, I rest,
close outer eyes
against elements gone wild.

Love, hate, dance, die.
howl, sing, crawl, fly:
the world I make conspires to overwhelm.

Doors open
behind closed eyes.
I breathe salvation, seed the storm.

I find, again, there is no-thing
I make or unmake, seek or flee,
that is not me.

I calm my self,
still the sea.
The night turns bright
with Deity.

ANNUNCIATION

**The angel of the Lord declared unto Mary,
and she conceived of the Holy Ghost**
The Angelus

Listen, friends, Romans, seekers,
to the familiar miracle;
memorized, recited, visualized,
each childhood noon.
Gabriel hovers. Mary bows her head.

Now I find the story is mine,
everyman's story of the call,
the summoning,
awakening of virgin psyche
to the seed of Spirit:
Truth descends to meet our need.

I feel the past rise up as gospel.
And if *I* attune to hear the song,
do I hear heaven…angel… intuition…
sounding in my heart?

I stretch my mind, feel God in me,
wake up, begin to see my inner, stature;
deeper, taller, angelic,
Christ born again each now
in me.

And
If I listen;
hear the call;
i n v i t e God in;
open to the seed of Spirit;

rejoice in the One I bear within;
nurture the Love living in my Heart;
bring Christ forth into the world each day;
allow my Christ, and yours, to grow, flourish;

raise up Peace with every thought;
feed on Joy in word and deed;
name it F r e e d o m,
name it G o d,
name *us*
God…

…what
wonders
can I then
create?

APPOINTMENT AT MACHU PICCHU

I rest upon an ancient terrace,
reach back in time and mind to see
the builders of this sacred city
Who made it for today...for me.

This journey first meant time and miles,
but ten days changed my heart and mind.
My consciousness, stretched wide to come,
left earth and time-bound me behind.

I trek the city up and down,
climb the walls to wonder how
archaic people built and filled
these ruined temples...empty now.

I lean my head on time-worn stone,
shed thinking, fill with energy,
the same it's ghostly priests had known.
It speaks again...this time, to me.

Lush blessings flow in air too thin.
I vow to sculpt my life anew.
Peaceful me makes peace on earth,
It flows from me as I *see* true.

I came miles to see a mountain,
but found the place where I can know:
I am my world's queen and priestess.
I rule and harvest what I sow.

I rest upon an ancient terrace,
content to feel what heaven means.
I am she who tends the flame
atop the mountain of my dreams.

AWAKENING

Something dropped away last night.
I'd felt it slipping for some time,
but could not name, or would not see,
the damaged piece, the not-right thing,
although I knew, unconsciously.

Would I put it on again,
pretty thing that meant so much?
What was that precious, needy part
that held me all together then?
I'd felt it changing in my heart.

Perhaps a part of my facade,
a costume worn to try my wings?
No, more a symbol of the past;
rite of passage, joy of youth,
dream of finding love that lasts.

Meaning came through loud and clear,
whole and seamless, right on time.
I tried to hide in busy-ness,
to sweep it under much-to-do.
I was afraid…I must confess.

Time stopped.
With a silent scream a "self" was gone;
mask of belonging I had grasped,
desire's sweet love-child,
need to have, to hold, to clasp.

Naked need, not strong enough
to bind that shiny self
to who-I-am,
when the dream of perfect love
turned out to be a sham.

I woke up, the mask slipped off,
I saw the world beyond my bed,
life beyond needs and fears,
past flesh and hunger.
Ego cried its bitter tears.

Was I sight-less, bound and gagged,
so enmeshed in want and need,
I could not open up and see?
Looking back, I know I was
where I was supposed to be.

Not that I will never pine
to long and belong,
open sweet but fleeting gifts.
But I have loved and lost before
and found that all but Spirit shifts.

Desire's reward still is sweet
though fading even as I grasp.
But I am so much more today,
whole and free, more real,
stronger than my mask.

When I love in time and space
I find the place where I am whole,
Know love is not in *that*, or you,
But alive and well in me,
always there, always true.

A love that lights the way for me,
where nothing's lost and all is gained,
where sharing self inspires no fear,
where I remember Who I Am
and why we come together here.

BECOMING ORCHESTRAL

**A tribute to the
American Chamber Orchestra
Prague - August, 2005**

When did I stop breathing?

Orchestra…
feast laid before me,
passion play,
holy communion.

Ordinary people,
tee shirted,
baseball capped,
don wings of music,
take up instruments,
fly,
make triumphant
symphonic love,
become heroes,
kings, goddesses,
seraphim.

No pale description,
no icy concept suffices.

Sacramental,
immortal concert;
drink the ensemble,
swallow the host.

Expletive completed:
notes made flesh,
exalted to flight,
lift,
dash, soar,
plummet,
glide serene,
flutter frantic in my head,
enhanced into being.

Mind mute with grandeur,
body rushes in to play,
court,
kiss,
embrace,
wed,
be born as
one more spirited instrument.

Feeling triumphs, expands
bubbles,
beggars thought.

Conducted elsewhere,
I become…

O R C H E S T R A L.

No need to breathe…
it breathes me.

Strange….
custom demands
I applaud only with my hands
in that breathless,
soul-tingling
moment after.

No one stands,
screams stomps, whistles,
waves a lighter….
(Inside me the crowd goes wild!)

BIGGER

Step out of darkness into noon.
Grope the familiar flash-blind, through white-hot spots.
Be Bambi frozen in the headlights of a celestial SUV.
See life awe-struck silver by Merlin's staff.
Dare eclipse bare-eyed, distant fire inviting risk.

Of course, adjustments can be made.

Pupils shrink,
arms fly up in protective salute,
glasses, visors, tiny holes in paper squares,
appear to slow the speed of light,
damp blazing glory,
mask naked alchemical wonder.

Careful now…don't hurt yourself!

Oh.
Too late.

Split moment of blind sight,
worlds of darkness drop away,
negative exposed.

You are bigger than your life.

You are the light.

DO IT ANYWAY: DONNA'S PRAYER

We journey ego-clouded ways,
and blind, think fear.
we do it anyway,
blindfolded by
a fog of illusions.

We give our will to God,
to the Universe,
to saving Grace.
We do it anyway,
in heartfelt confidence,
trust the seer inside.

Challenge leads the way home,
guides, corrects our course.
We do it every day,
in fear's dark afternoon,
through nightmare,
toward the light.

Fear transforms,
corrals us to green pastures.
We do it as the way,
reach for the light within,
illumine the world,
shine the way back home.

CALLING IN

I call out
God!
in the night,
seek comfort elsewhere,
pin hopes on ancestral yearnings:
come up empty.

Despair calls out
Help me!
hurls energy upward to
where aid is vaguely felt to be:
nobody home.

I call out in anguish
Why me?
curse the hand that feeds,
arms that cherish and protect:
my God! (is dead)

I call out
Save me...I'm melting!
feel the crumble of dissolving myth,
fractured fairy tale:
the wizard snores.

I cease calling,
spent, heart-sick.
Shrouded in silence, I give up.
Defenses breached, I surrender:
God is there.

Spirited Light
pierces darkness,
calms troubled water,
frees captive heart..
I wake up.

Think again,
See,
open wide the gate of divinity,
to where God is
breathing me.

Now I call infor God
if storms and monsters rage and roar.
I live love, give love, am love.
God is all I see.

COME AWAY

Come away, they said,
come away from the flames.
The fire is hot,
you'll burn yourself up.
Don't stand so close, come away!

Come away, they said,
come away from the sea.
The water is deep,
you'll fall in and drown.
Don't play on the shore, come away!

Come away, they said,
come away from the earth.
You'll be buried alive,
lost in the pit.
Don't stand on the edge, come away!

Come away, they said,
come away from the storm.
You'll be swept away,
Better run, better hide.
Don't stand out there, come away!

Inside the fire,
I'm naked to Self.
Phoenix rises,
ego burns clear.

Flow healing water,
dissolve my illusions,
wash me transparent
to see who I Am.

Close to the earth,
I till holy ground,
fertile Self blossoming
in toward the Light.

Riding the tempest,
doubt blows away.
I breathe a new world
from the I of the storm.

Come away, they said.
Don't stand so close.
But I did

kiss the flame,
ride the storm,
wed the earth,
walk the sea.

Burnt …I am pure.
Blown clear…I fly free.
Buried…I rise.
Cleansed…I Am Me.

FALLEN ANGEL

I was taking down the Christmas tree,
reaching round in back
I bumped the tree (and rocked my world).
That's when I heard a crash.

The angel lay upon the tile
knocked down from way up high;
ceramic face, ceramic floor.
I thought I heard her cry.

All golden robes and golden wings,
faceless, up she gazed.
I looked at her…and held my breath,
looked *in,* and was amazed.

No moan, no gasp, no expletive
escaped my lips that day.
I saw a message on that floor
to guide me on my way.

She had no mouth to shout at me,
but I heard, *Stop and hear!*
Her shattered eyes beamed light and love,
I *felt* it, loud and clear.

She told me what I need to know:
Beware the little me!
Look with more than human sight
if I would truly see.

Be sure I hear with Spirit's ears
the music for my dance.
Face and form are fragile things,
prone to happenstance.

I breathed *a-ha*... quietly.
I did not make a fuss.
But no one now can tell me that
God does not speak to us.

I lovingly repaired her head,
the old replaced with new,
and each day try to do the same
in all I think and do.

I thank my fallen angel-guide.
I thank my yuletide tree.
and daily live the lesson taught
that Christmastime to me.

GOD IN MY GLASS

Wine,
glorious fermented fruit,
makes me feel
...*blessed.*

Crisp white, soft red,
unpretentious wine-in-a-box;
loosens tongue, body,
layered civility.

Wellbeing rises
s l o w l y...
seductively, in the blood,
paints rosy landscapes,
fascinating friends,
undying love.

I select, buy,
pour, hold it up to the light,
look, tip, look again,
swirl, sniff, sip, (don't swallow)
savor, (now swallow).

Judge nose, legs, clarity, flavor
(semi-dry, overtones of raspberry,
peach and pepper, with an oak-y finish).

As I've grown, I've made peace with wine,
like ego, re-considered,
re-prioritized,
moderated, gentled.

The two are partners, bonded, buddies:
ego in a glass;
wine poured into the cup of separation,
counted on to free, enhance, shine,
hide.

Now I free, enhance, shine myself.
Nothing to hide,
I sip surrender
(freedom: overtones of wholeness,
sweetness and light, with a peaceful finish).

Wine,
glorious fermented fruit,
makes me feel blessed;
swirls pale gold,
translucent ruby,
in my glass…

and I taste God.

HAPPY NOW

A woman channels Jesus?
Yes, of course, I'll go.
Sometimes I still look outside,
Forgetting that I know.

She said I get one question.
What did I want to I learn?
The question had to be just right,
one that really burns.

WHAT WILL I BE WHEN I GROW UP?

Oh No! I'd planned to ask him how
to set our spirits free,
to ask what life is all about,
not something about me!

The question is too trivial,
I didn't use my head.
But then,
NO QUESTION IS TOO TRIVIAL,
He said.

Jesus! What was I thinking
to sound so incomplete?
But though I thought I'd missed my chance,
he didn't miss a beat.

While I was wishing I'd asked how
to save humanity,
He smiled serenely, held my gaze...
all He said was
HAPPY.

HAPPY? Is that it?
Whatever does it mean?
I want lots of details.
Paint me the whole scene.

I blurted out,
OK, WHEN?
That's all my pride allowed.
Still serene, He looked at me,
and only answered
NOW.

I felt put down, deflated,
and wallowed in that feeling
while insights happened all around me,
breakthroughs, tears and healing.

I was stuck at...*HAPPY.*
What was that all about?
In all that sacred energy,
why was I left out?

HAPPY?!

Of course, his answer was the
right and perfect one for me.
My upset rose from thinking,
from not *feeling,* what to be.

The problem is I think too much,
and think I have to *do,*
when happiness is knowing from
my heart Source what is true.

The answer is so short and sweet,
just like Jesus said.
But I had never looked too close
at where His teachings led.

Now I see, if He is God
then I must be God too.
And *being God's* the only thing
I really have to do.

Each precious day,
HAPPY NOW
is all I seek to be,
although who said it matters not
so very much to me.

I open up right now to hear
what Spirit has to say,
and bless whatever messenger
speaks truth to me today.

RIDING THE GREAT WHITE

Summarily tossed in my fragile vessel,
I plunge seas of archaic thought,
whirlpools of orthodoxy,
turbulent vain imaginings.

Dashed on reefs of rhetoric,
I drown to ephemeral life,
sink graceful,
grateful,
into silver-green silence,
sway, languorous with
mellifluous metaphysics.

Washed crystalline
I float free,
healed at depth by currents of Love,
geysers of Truth, tidal waves of Joy.

Pristine
I rise on the spume of Spirit,
ride the Great White of God Mind
bareback ,
whisper foamy salutations,
create oceans of meaning in my wake.

IN RELUCTANT PRAISE OF BIBLE STUDY

Yea, verily, I say unto you.

I have walked through the valley
of the shadow of doubt,
wrestled with words, angels and demons,
been fed by gospels of men,
and stories of Jesus.

I've been drunk with Noah,
gleaned with Ruth,
bowled three games with Joseph and his brothers,
dredged metaphysical meaning
from morning mist.

I've chased Jacob and his kin
through deceit to triumph,
through famine to plenty,
through slavery to liberation, and back.
I've met myself in his world
both coming in and going out.

I've trashed a holy book,
buried a dreaded icon,
uncovered a transcendent myth,
minced the living word.

I've been frustrated, disgusted,
edified, awed, and (yes)
excited.

I've met folks like me,
who love and lie,
give life, take it,
fall down, rise up,
get lost, find themselves,
who, like me,
must choose:
compete
or
be complete
with God.

I've gone kicking and questioning
into the Promised Land,
from Eden, to Palestine, to Egypt,
and found myself…home,
in a land of milk and cookies.

I was impressed.

But one last question…

…rather like *THE WIZARD OF OZ,*
Don't you think?

PIECES OF YOU

Oh my God,
Look at me!
I chop the world in two.

Slice and dice,
split hairs, mince words,
until I splinter You.

King and peon,
idol, fan,
genius, jester,
shaman, sham.

Goodwife, mistress,
boss man, bum,
hero, houseboy,
cream and scum.

Merlin, mountebank,
savior, saved,
lord and lackey
master, slave.

Lost in parts,
I miss the whole,
decorate my half-a-soul.

Drowned in separate,
can't see the One,
I reach for more 'till I'm undone.

Oh my God,
I see it now,
lost in space, and running wild,

I crash and burn until I *see*:
I am the Christ -
the only Child

Oh my God,
I now affirm
I will chop no more.

I'll celebrate
not separate
the One I'm looking for.

QUEEN OF HEARTS

I was
(blind, deaf, numb),
could not fathom life past
supper,
shelter,
sex.

But I am
the Queen of Hearts.
I rule how I see.

So off with my head!
Out gushes fear and doubt,
blown away on winds of change.

Headless,
I am free.

I open:
clear, clean,
empty,
fullfill-able,
fresh-cut me.

Spirit walks in,
plants Itself,
sprouts new *God-ness*,
blooms,
opens its eye.

I see,
look into the
bleeding hearts of the matter,
find
only One.

I
am the
headless
horsewoman
of my apocalypse,
singing my timely demise,
dancing the new world
as it flows
out from
me.

SATIS

**An interpretation of the message of
Mel Gibson's film, *The Passion Of The Christ*.
"Satis", spoken to the soldiers scourging Jesus,
means roughly, " enough."**

SATIS!
My soul cries, enough!
Quite enough of scourging crucifying fear.
If this cup cannot pass away,
taste grape,
not gall.

SATIS!
Enough, already!
Enough of enemies: Jew, gentile,
Roman, barbarian, faithful, infidel.
Children: love one another.
Celebrate diversity.

SATIS!
Soldier, enough of war,
death and weeping widows!
Sweet mother, nurture.
Mary, love. Wise Claudia, counsel.
Veronica, dry our tears.

SATIS!
It is past time, my gods!
Yahweh, Allah, Isis, Great Spirit,
Unite: not gods, but *god-ness*.
Choose no contest,
God in all.

SATIS!
It is accomplished!
when we discard the dregs
serve the good wine, see one vine,
fill the half full cup,
drink to Who-We-Are.

SATIS!
Our spirit cries, enough!
God of love and forgiveness,
flow through us into the world.
Gladly we let go of cross and shroud
and we rise.

THE QUESTION

I stare into my fridge,
bare bulb lighting what I've got,
shelves of what I do not want.
Still, I get to choose, or not.

What is this urgent, burning hunger
That cries out loud in my gut?
Do this, do that, hide the craving
for, oh God, I don't know what.

What to feel, to love, to buy?
Sweet, salt, sour, shudder, sex, and spend.
Am I filled with all this having?
No, I'm not: I find it never ends.

Do I, snake-like, grab and eat my tail?
Gorge on mirrors, smoke and taste?
Chew holes in knowing? All the while
unfed by person, thing or place.

At night in dreams I search
where reason crosses soul's desire.
Moon lights up dry seas and bottles
that don't quench thirst or dowse the fire.

Camping on the brink of hopeless,
edge of not enough and way too much,
I brush the verge of ancient, ardent stillness.
Frantically, the ego cries, *Don't touch!*

In silence I choose freedom now
in what I think, and say and do.
God-self shines on inner stores
where I am fed on what is true.

I look into my life today,
choose gratitude for what I've got;
fill full of essence, presence, peace.
From here I choose to Be,
or not.

WANTING LESS

Of late, I feel my doings
with humanity are strained.
The banter, laughter, platitudes,
the pleasantries are pained.

The gloss, the glitter, song and dance,
which used to be my joy
feel flat, tasteless, not-me now.
They seem a tired ploy.

It's odd. I find I'm wanting less:
less stuff, less sound, less talk;
less of loveless making love,
more tending to the flock,

less touchy-feely feeling less,
more digging way down deep,
less common-place unkindness,
more nights when I can sleep,

Less walling off my true self,
more true selves to greet,
less *us* making war on *them,*
more *halfway-theres* to meet.

The old amusements don't amuse.
I trash my sad old stories,
weep farewell to childhood dreams,
wave *bye* to faded glories.

Downsize, clean house, simplify,
until I am set free.
Let loose the butterfly inside
to live exquisitely.

Yes, my small self still feels stressed
by others in the hive.
But how they grow when I let go,
the whole world comes alive.

Less is more and more is less:
that's my new attitude.
I live to grow into the flow
and practice gratitude.

WASHING DAD

First there were three:
my love, my Dad, and I,
bonded by near deaths, altered states,
born-again selves.

Husband and father laid low,
then lifted up by strokes of fate.
Related in-law and by unmanly disability:
second father, first son, daughter-wife.

Stroke-bound brothers:
one found new life in caring,
one the son he never had,
and I, a family of three.

Then there were two.
As if wifely grief were not enough,
I got to fill empty arms
with withered, fragile, father-flesh
and, drowning old paradigms…wash him.

No hiding from this
final dissonance.
I soaped and scrubbed, and dried
the loins that gave me life.

He cried, helpless, shivering,
raging impotent,
against the cold
and choice-less age.

Nearer the end, all dignities aside,
me, stripped to shorts and tee,
Dad, pale trembling flesh In the shower,
wet with water and filial tears: our finest hour.

Time circled around as he clung to me,,
afraid to fall.
(Remembering... my first two-wheeler:
he ran beside, held me up
when I was afraid to fall).

New divinity discovered,
unsought, un-thought,
worlds away from where we were:
my Father, naked in the shower.
God uncovered.

Childhood upside-down,
parenthood reversed,
meaning that, childless, I never hoped to know:
redeemed, re-born
...washing Dad.

WHAT TO DO?

What do I do with that old time religion
when I know that I am God?

Collective un-conscious, tides of community,
nudge me to worship.

I strive mightily to see beyond
a world I wish to rise above.

It rears its head, alive and well:
kicks me.

Immanence breathes hot
on the heels of transcendence.

Shadowy form tangos seductively
across the ceiling of my inner focus.

Now I fathom fire, flood, famine:
not to punish, but to rock loose,
slap awake, snap back
from frantic trance.

What to do?

Wash my child with water,
chant Om, tone amen,
shout halleluiah, dance the seasons;

light candles, pyres, torches;
walk stations, labyrinths, fire;
offer flesh, flowers, gold;

journey to Mecca, Jerusalem, Rome,
sacred city, holy river,
magic mountain, wailing wall;

build mounds, temples, mosques,
synagogues, churches, bingo halls;
tend oak groves, sacred springs;

spin wheels, finger beads, ring bells,
drink blood, swallow hosts, revere cattle;
slay devils, virgins, goats, the infidel;

whirl entranced, bow to the east;
sit shiva, lotus, silent;
hug a tree, save the earth.

Surrender in frustration, celebration, awe.

Remember
The
Mystery.

Part Four

I Am The One

When I quantify space I create time....
When I quantify time I create space....
When I quantify myself I create a person.

Deepak Chopra
The Book Of Secrets

You are the truth from foot to brow.
Now what else would you like to know?

Rumi
in
365 Nirvana Here and Now

To know yourself as
the being underneath the thinker,
the stillness underneath the mental noise,
the love and joy beneath the pain,
is freedom, salvation,
enlightenment.

Eckhart Tolle
The Power of Now

PAINTING PEACE

Mind is a brush
coloring life,
picturing worlds
in love or in strife.

Inspired by Spirit,
we see Love increase
lives colored Joy,
worlds painted Peace.

I AM, AREN'T I?

God within
All-That-Is
Great I AM
(it's me)

You are
(in here)
somewhere
out there
(all-where)

center point on which I stand
essence from which I create
power point from which I fly
sky from which I fall to earth

sneezing symphonies
coughing kingdoms
blazing guts and glory

from my staff
my wand
my prolific word

in the blink of a thought
twinkle of an idea
fate-full turn of time

You live me into being
(don't You?)
in the breathless
space between thoughts

I live You into being
(don't I?)
Small gods and heroes rise and fall
pale at Your boundlessness
disappear in our
infinite internal landscape

Nietzsche says
You are dead
(are You?)

I dance a lusty *No!*
sing a hearty *Yes!*
in joy,
in love
where we are
One

You Are
therefore I Am
(tell Descartes!)

it is so.

YOU ARE: I AM

You Are:
Mother, heart-mind,
nature, nurture,
blood and home.

You Are:
Father, guardian,
maker, breaker,
sword and bone.

You Are:
sister, brother,
deathless daughter,
rising son.

You Are:
all and no-thing,
self-less Being,
All in One.

You Are (I Am):
wave of Godhood,
piece of One Mind,
good and true.

You Are (I Am):
breathing Life.
Speak, and mountain
moves for You.

We
A r e.
Ask, receiving.
Seek and find it.
Knock and open up.

We do.

NOW WHEN

Salute the fertile past.
Honor way-back-when.
Rich emergent
field of dreams,
births now and also, then.

Receive the gifts of now:
love rises to our need.
We conceive
the infinite,
become the future's seed.

High watch for what-will-be,
a child expecting Dad:
unsure what
great gift will come,
but sure good will be had.

Create our Heaven here.
Love now, live as Source.
Harvest blessings
from what-is
and plant for more,
of course.

STORM SONG

We are
divine order:
eye of the storm,
troops at our border.

Still
inside,
God protects,
saves,

unassailable,
p a t I e n t;
as
children scream,
and soldiers moan,
mama!

Waiting:
deity abides
while we
ride wind and war,

until we change
our minds.

JUST FOR ME

Tonight the moon rose just for me,
shone above a cloud-crowned sea,
illuminated heart and soul,
celestial splendor...just for me.

Tonight stars glittered just for me,
sky Disney-domed over silver sea,
twinkled in my small, small world,
heaven's marvels...just for me.

Tonight the wind played just with me,
on skin and hair, fresh from the sea.
It stroked and teased, caressed my soul;
a natural wonder...just for me.

Tonight the surf rolled just for me.
In foamy ranks the awesome sea
rushed to my feet and washed away
my separate self...the earth-bound me.

Tonight the sky and wind and waves
became my world, my way, my me.
My inner being shone out my life.
I breathed the wind...I *was* the sea.

I was emptied, filled, reborn;
drawn in, and up, and out, to see;
freed to trust, to feel, to know…
all is One…all is me.

Today the waves break just for me,
Unfurling from an endless sea,
uncovering sands I've never walked,
the sacred shores inside of me.

SACRED ME

I came close, then ran away,
shy around the sacred Me.
I did not know just who-I-am,
I feared to open up and see.

Helping others heal each day
did not touch my heart.
But when I met the God in me,
I found my missing part.

I felt and saw past worldly ways
stepped in the flow, learned how to *be*.
Now I deny my loss and fear,
see only love when I claim Me.

I come up close to God and stay,
embrace the Source that sets me free.
I know just Who I (Really) Am.
I love and live sacred Me.

EXCLAIM!

Spirit in me is me.
It's true!

I fired my ego.
Out it flew!

I shouted,
Hey you, don't you think me!

I won't hide my True Self.
I'm free!

I choose God-Is.
I take my stand!

Celebrate now!
I live
I Am!

THERE AND BACK

The three of us are one, we are,
you and I and Spirit;
all bound up together here,
as we learn not to fear it.

We flow out to everything
from Godhead's fiery heart,
exploding Love into the world,
to every blessed part.

You redeem the Universe
as you see God in me,
and when I learn to heal myself
I can set you free.

We trace our glowing embers back,
be still and know it's done,
to meet God in the heartland where
we three become
the One.

VASE

crystal
clear
Absolute,
contains the
water of Life,
nurturIng
ephemeral
blossoms of
exquIsIte
fleetIng
form.
It is so.

Part Five

Prayers, Songs and Blessings

...the spiritual
is not something that happens
when there are paranormal phenomena,
or in a church...or any one of the glorified
pilgrimage sites that seduce the New Ager.
In fact, the sacred is everywhere.
The sacred is everything.
And every one is part of
a sacred process.

Richard Moss
in
365 Nirvana Here And Now

The process of prayer becomes much easier when,
rather than having to believe that
God will always say yes to every request,
one understands intuitively that
the request itself is not necessary.

Neal Donald Walsh
Meditations From Conversations With God: Book 1

God pours through every moment,
every blade of grass,
every flash of a human eye.
But to see this
you have to hold yourself lightly,
because if you are too attached
to your fears, your anger, your shame,
then all you can see is yourself.
The universe jitterbugs past,
all the presence of God manifest...
while you sit in the corner
whining about your life.

James A. Connor
in
365 Nirvana Here And Now

ALL WAYS AFFIRMATIONS

Know the Light: think the One

Feel the Light: fall into Love.

See the Light: perceive us One.

Bear the Light: birth the Christ.

Hold the Light: affirm we are.

Share the Light: speak the word.

Feed the Light: love and forgive.

Shine the Light: serve and remember.

Be the Light: live it so.

And it Is.

ANGEL LOVE: MICHAEL'S SONG

Go within when you are blue.
Angel Love will come to you.

Peace, be still…think of God,
if ever you feel sad or odd.

You will feel the peace inside
when your heart is open wide.

Light and Strength come forth to lead
you back to knowing what you need.

Back to knowing that you are
complete just being *you*, a star,

Spirit, in whom Love abides
whatever storms may rage outside.

Angel Love prepares the way
for Joy to bless you every day.

Be content, know you are whole,
and let your Angel Self unfold.

BLESS THIS HOUSE

Bless this house, dear friends, today,
as we meet to find our way.
Make a haven from the storm,
where we can gather safe and warm,

where we come to know our Source,
where our woes may run their course.
Make a place to learn and grow
to be, to love, to fly, to flow.

Make a place where we rejoice,
where we can hear each other's voice,
where music plays and dancers dance,
and we may meet our God, perchance.

Bless my house, dear friends, each day
that we discuss, and laugh and pray.
Create a space where Spirit sings.
Give thanks for what each presence brings.

God bless this house, O Lord I pray,
and all the friends who come today.

CHANT

**Back to your childhood for this one:
jumping rope, bouncing balls,
hopscotch, jacks,
one potato…**

It's all Good
Goody good good
Good good
Goody good
Good God
Whee!

It's all God
Goody good God
Good God
Goody God
Good God
Be!

It's all One
Goody, two, three
One God
Goody God
One, two
Me!

It's all Good
Goody God me
Good God
Goody me
One, two
Free!

God is all
Goody good Be
All God
Goody God
ready, set
Whee!

AFFIRMATIONS FOR A CHURCH

Hold us, Mother:
Love, nurture, embrace, accept,
feed us God, wrap us in grace,
draw Spirit out from within.

Lead us, Father:
strong, firm, purposeful,
tender shepherd, wise steward,
seed of Spirit, sword of truth.

Fall into Love with us.
Hold grace's mirror that we may see
the beauty in ourselves.
Share the truth that leads us home.

Shelter God's children:
a place to start, grow, rest, re-charge;
turf, touchstone, haven, hearth,
heart.

Baptize with belonging,
heal with forgiveness,
songs of love, dance of fellowship
sacrament of stillness.

We greet our selves in you:
connect, process, practice,
walk the path to Source and Self,
whole and holy.

Through Grace we are drawn here,
awaken and love, here,
are born again, healed,
go forth to create the Kingdom.

We are grateful that it is so.

GODDESS BIRTHDAY PRAYER

Goddess bless and bring you joy,
laughter, love, and life.
Goddess grant and Goddess give
serenity through strife.

Her arms are raised to shine the Light
on each and every task.
Her Spirit rises strong in you
if only you will ask.

She tempers might with wisdom,
leads you straight and true.
Unites in love with Father God
to heal and balance you.

Goddess blessings on your day:
A smile upon your face.
Be born anew each year, each now,
walk free in Light and Grace.

HAIL WOMAN

Hail woman,
full of grace,
the Goddess is you.
Blessed are you,
beloved of Spirit,
and blessed is the Christ
you bear to the world.
Holy woman,
Mother of Love,
nurture our Oneness,
now
and each hour of our life.

Amen.

I DO

Our Father Who Art , Great I Am,
can You come out and play?
You can, we can,
I can, I trust my life
to You today.

Oh Sweet Goddess, Mother Earth,
work with me right now.
You can, we can,
I can when I say *Yes!*
and don't ask how.

Oh Eternal All-That-Is,
give us your peace on earth.
You can, we can,
I make my peace,
affirming each one's worth.

Jehovah, Allah, El-Shaddai,
bring on your Kingdom Come.
You can, we can,
I can when I
see all of us as One.

Holy Spirit, Sacred Tao,
calm my seas today.
You will, we will
I will when God
is all I think and say.

Divinity walks in my shoes.
These questions are for me.
I live the answers
when I know
it's God I need to be.

LITANY I: MOTHER GOD

Mother-God
I affirm
our wisdom and strength
each day
I live my sacred woman's way:

ruling: nations, home, and heart;

giving birth, defying death;

open womb, open arms;

making love, money, waves,
motherhood and apple pie;

un-making war, waging peace;

loving tender, loving tough;

healing body, mind, and soul;

master of logic, mistress of magic;

flying high, close to the earth;

raising children, hope, and hell;

    taming the beast,
    leading it Home.

    I am your Tree of Life.

    I live You as I create,
    re-membering
    your world
with our love children.

        I proclaim
      what we make
        together
          good…
        beautiful:

          It is so.

before
        now
                forever

LITANY II: ONE WOMAN

We are
one woman
all women

earth-soul, heart-mind
shakti-she, sweet sword

femina dei, dea mundi
world builder, bridge weaver

root of family, milk of nations
breeding life, bleeding love

drawing love
from heaven above
flowing love
from heaven inside

lantern on the face of God
beacon for the heart of man

all women
one woman
we are
so.

LABYRINTH PRAYER

I walk in to where I AM
and out to where we are.
Refreshed, renewed, I wake up
to walk my talk, raise the bar.

I fill with strength each day
that God is my recourse.
I go within to seek the One,
releasing all to Source.

I touch the holy hem of Truth,
open up to Love,
allow my self to know God is
inside and not above.

I breathe Spirit's peace and joy,
feel Light and whole and free.
I seek the Way, the Life, the Truth
and find them all in me.

OUR SOURCE I

Our Source,
Who is our Substance

Holy are Your Names,

Your kingdom is here
in us, as us,
not separate from us,
as we live our divine nature.

Your Will is ours
as we choose the One,
Divine Order,
unfolding Life.

Good sufficient for the day
flows to us, through us:
constant Grace
holy communion.

You are Love,
blood of divine kinship,
flowing even when we forget,

as we affirm divine kinship,
when the family of man forgets.

Our
Oneness
guides, strengthens,
sustains,
saves,
in the face of
challenge, crisis, chaos:
all God.

We live
Your power and glory
forever,
choose heaven

Now.

And here it is.

OUR SOURCE II

Our
Source,
Core of Being,
Holy are our names.

I open to our present Oneness,
surrender to the flow of Divinity which
I manifest on earth, as You manifest us.

I am affirmed, nurtured, sustained in every moment,
as I affirm, nurture, and sustain all of creation

in remembrance of our common D I v I n I t y.

Chaos and challenge have no power in my True
Being, for at depth I am whole and sacred,
expressing S o u r c e, here and now.

I have my wisdom, my power,
my g l o r y, in our
O N E N E S S,
f o r e v e r:
N O W.
Yes!

OFFERING

Today
we live our
thanksgiving for the
constant grace of God's Presence
in our lives, and In our life together here.

We are filled-with Your gifts, all good, all God.

We are Your Circle of Life: fertile ground...seed of
possibility...abundant harvest...fallow field.

We give what is ours alone to give, from
our divinely ordered place, receive
as we release, heal our world,
celebrate Who-we-are,
remember our
One Life.

Today
we live our
thanksgiving.
We are blessed. It is so.

PRAYER FOR LIVING

Source Energy ,
we join at the Heart,
to meet each other
in the heaven of possibilities.

We rest,
recharge…en-lighten,
open to present Wisdom,
enhance one another through
our divine connection.

We give thanks,
fill with constant grace,
Divine Love,
which knits time bound experience
into coherence.

We bless
delight and crisis,
wonder and challenge,
synchronicity and chaos,
precious gifts, holy process,
timeless Life unfolding:
which is You,
which is us.

We open to
seeing and hearing You,
talking and walking You,
living You,
being You.

We feast on the
bread of fellowship,
bless earth,
build heaven,
breathe Spirit,
live Truth.

We are grateful
that
it is so.

RELATIONSHIP INVOCATION

Oh
Divine Love!
Breathe joy,
sigh challenge,
multiply blessings,
maximize the lessons we
provide each other
as we try to touch
the place where
WE ARE ONE.
YES!

SEAMLESS: TOM'S SONG

We make our gods so seamlessly,
as nature, judge, as Christ or king;
then we come to judge ourselves
as what we've made, as God or thing.

We think our gods out of the sky,
raise them up, then cry in fright:
Who and how and why am I here?
God, oh God, where is the Light?

We clasp ourselves with empty arms,
and caught in thinking fear, despair,
until we wake, look *in,* and see
that God, indeed, burns brightly there

We see God in the seamless we.
We find ourselves in Deity.
We circle 'round and 'round until
we let our struggles go and *Be.*

<u>Chorus</u>: Seamless, seamlessly,
we are lanterns for God's pure Light,
Seamless, seamlessly,
we're beacons leading Home.

(Music: Janine Chimera 5/04)

SINGING YOU HOME: A CELEBRATION

Clan gathers around
to mourn its loss;
our kin, our mate, our friend, our dear.

We draw close, inward,
to heal our wounded heart
in the warmth of family,
tend the wound your passing leaves,
affirm your eternal Life,
and our continuity.

You are gone,
but the Love you made
lives on as family.

It lives in us:
in children, in face and form,
in blood, in-law, in memory;
in friend, in deed, in story;
in the love which will flourish,
all unattended,
when we who remember
are gone.

Today we gather
to sing you on your way.

Can you feel them drawing near?
Dearly beloveds, gone before,
who join us again to lead you home:
parents, grand and great,
partners, friends,
all the ones who led the way
to where we are today,
here…now.

We are complete in love.
Though grieving fills us
we rejoice that you are
whole and free once more.

Now,
love and farewell.
You live forever in our hearts.

And welcome home
to that perfect place
where there is
only love.

THE OVERFLOWING CUP

I intend to experience the **Presence of God**

I ask to experience **the P r e s e n c e of God**

I open to **experience the Presence of God**

I **allow my experience the Presence of God**

I e x p e r i e n c e the Presence of God

I experience the P r e s e n c e

I experience GOD

I Am the

Presence

I Am

GOD

( )

AM

aaaaahhhhhhhhhhhh

WEDDING SONG

I joyfully affirm
your
Conscious Partnership.
which
blesses and enhances
the depth of your Loving
the length of your Living
the breadth of your Laughter
the window of your possibilities

I solemnly affirm
your
eternal Connection
with Spirit
which
guides you through
abundant opportunities
for love, growth, and service,
as together
you create
your
Kingdom of Heaven.

It is good and true.
It is so!

LITANY III: WOMAN PRAYER

I open to God within: I am nurtured.

I walk on water toward my Self: I step out in Joy.

I drink the cup of Love: I am strengthened.

I soar on wings of Spirit: I raise my consciousness.

My sisters are my heart: I am cherished.

My brothers comfort me: I share the Love.

Spirit's abundance pours through me:
I breathe peace and plenty.

My Light defies the darkness: I illuminate.

I express the will of God: life unfolds before me.

I am Divine Order: there are no mistakes.

I allow Source to express me: I walk in Grace forever.

I do.

EPILOGUE

MEMORIAL FOR THE AUTHOR

Maggie: child of Spirit,
beloved of God,
survived by love.

Consummated not gone,
home not lost,

Released not grasped,
celebrated not mourned,

Shaken not stirred
by life.

Laugh, don't cry.
Dance, don't stop.
Sing! Don't *sshhhh!*

Respectfully remembered
by family, friends, lovers,
colleagues, acquaintances,
beloved adversaries;
familiar, once, and never-met.

Encountered in body, word, and mind;
holy intercourse, human communion,
heartfelt embrace, service, prayer…
…the silence.

We all say
she touched me,
here…and here…
where I feel;

Called my best self out to play,
made me think again,

twist and shout,
giggle, laugh, snort,

curse mightily,
cry shamelessly,

dance my dance,
pray my prayer;

Created beauty where she lived,
with hands and heart,
mouth and mind,
arms and spirit;

Sifted, simmered, savored
the joy and pain of life,
served gutsy sustenance
for body and soul;

Celebrate a self
used up in the now that was.

Nothing left but memories,
love prints
in the time of her life.

No regrets.
Oh…
maybe not loving herself more,
first;

and that old confusion,
loving too much
or not enough,
now dissolved in Spirit.

Take what's left of her
often multiplied
loaves and fishes.

Feed the beloveds
who do God's work.

Buy dancing shoes
for the trudging world.

Eat.

Drink.

Touch.

Love.

Yes!

BENEDICTION

May I be at peace.
May the world be at peace.

May I have an open heart.
May we all have an open heart.

May I know the beauty of my true nature.
May we all know the beauty of our true nature.

May I be healed.
May we all be healed.

May my life be a gift of peace in the world.
May we all serve as a gift of peace to each other.

Within each heart is a place of peace.
May we each live from that place.

And thus we are healed into the heart of peace.

Marina Raye
Prayer For Peace
CD jacket
Liquid Silk

SOURCES AND INSPIRATIONS

A Course in Miracles and selected Miracle Studies material,
The Song Of Prayer, Foundation For Inner Peace - 1978
Journey Beyond Words and ***The Other Voice***, Brent Haskell; DeVorss Press -1997
Miracle Cards

Robert Brumet
Finding Yourself In Transition, Unity House - 2001

Deepak Chopra
The Book of Secrets; Harmony Books - 2004
Everyday Immortality, Harmony Books - 1999

Wayne Dyer,
The Power Of Intention, Hay House - 2004

Myrtle Fillmore
Healing Letters, Unity School of Christianity

James Dillet Freeman
Love Is Strong as Death, Unity House – 2000

Esther and Jerry Hicks
Ask And It Is Given: Learning To Manifest Your Desires (The Teachings of Abraham), Hay House - 2004

Kryon: Book Eight – 2000 Passing the Marker (Understanding the New Millennium Energy; The Kryon Writings, Inc. – 2000

Mules Of Love: Poems By Ellen Bass, BOA Editions, Ltd. – 2002

Wayne Muller
How Then Shall We Live? Bantam Books - 1996
Learning To Pray: How We Find Heaven on Earth, Bantam books - 2000

Penney Peirce
The Present Moment: A Daybook Of Clarity And Intuition, Contemporary Books – 2000

Marina Raye
Liquid Silk…Journey into the Heart of Peace, Native Heart Music -1999

Gary R. Renard
The Disappearance of the Universe: Straight Talk About Illusions, Past lives, Religion, Sex Politics, and the Miracles of Forgiveness, Fearless books - 2003

Mattie J.T. Stepanek
Hope Through Heartsongs, Hyperion Press - 2002
Journey Through Heartsongs, Hyperion Press 200

The Essential Rumi
translations by Coleman Barks, Castle Books - 1997

The Gift: Poems by Hafiz The Great Sufi Master,
translations by Daniel Ladinsky; Penguin Compass - 1999

The Impersonal Life, DeVorss and Co. - 1983
(Joseph Benner)

365 Nirvana Here And Now: Living Every Moment In Enlightenment*, Josh* Baran, editor; Element - 2003

Eckhardt Tolle
The Power of Now, New World Library - 1999
Practicing the Power of Now, New World Library - 2001

Neal Donald Walsh
Meditations from Conversations With God: An Uncommon Dialogue Book I, Berkeley Books - 1997
Communion With God, Random House - 2000
What God Wants, Atria Books -2005
The New Revelation, Atria Books - 2004
Tomorrow's God, Atria Books - 2002